HOT and COLD

Nicolas Brasch

Australia • Brazil • Japan • Korea • Mexico • Singapore • Spain • United Kingdom • United States

Hot and Cold

Fast Forward
Yellow Level 8

Text: Nicolas Brasch
Illustrations: Boris Silvestri
Editor: Johanna Rohan
Design: James Lowe
Series design: James Lowe
Production controller: Hanako Smith
Photo research: Corrina Tauschke
Audio recordings: Juliet Hill, Picture Start
Spoken by: Matthew King and Abbe Holmes
Reprint: Jennifer Foo

Acknowledgements
The author and publisher would like to acknowledge permission to reproduce material from the following sources: Photographs by APL/Corbis/Robert Weight/Ecoscene, p. 15; Lindsay Edwards, back cover, pp. 4-5; Photo Edit/David Young-Wolff, p. 11; Photolibrary.com/Rick Price, pp. 10, 13/ Superstock, Inc., p. 10 inset/ Photolibrary.com/Age foto stock/Frank Krahmer, p. 12/ Photolibrary.com/Science Photo Library/Doug Allan, cover bottom.

ISBN 978 0 17 012518 5
ISBN 978 0 17 012513 0 (set)

Cengage Learning Australia
Level 7, 80 Dorcas Street
South Melbourne, Victoria Australia 3205
Phone: 1300 790 853

Cengage Learning New Zealand
Unit 4B Rosedale Office Park
331 Rosedale Road, Albany, North Shore NZ 0632
Phone: 0508 635 766

For learning solutions, visit **cengage.com.au**

Printed in Australia by Ligare Pty Ltd
9 10 11 12 13 14 15 22 21 20 19 18

THE UNIVERSITY OF MELBOURNE

Evaluated in independent research by staff from the Department of Language, Literacy and Arts Education at the University of Melbourne.

Nicolas Brasch

Contents

Chapter 1

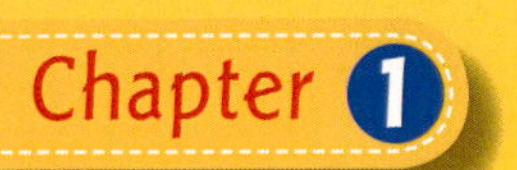

WHAT IS TEMPERATURE?

Temperature is the measure of how hot or cold something is.

Some people look at the TV to hear the air temperature.

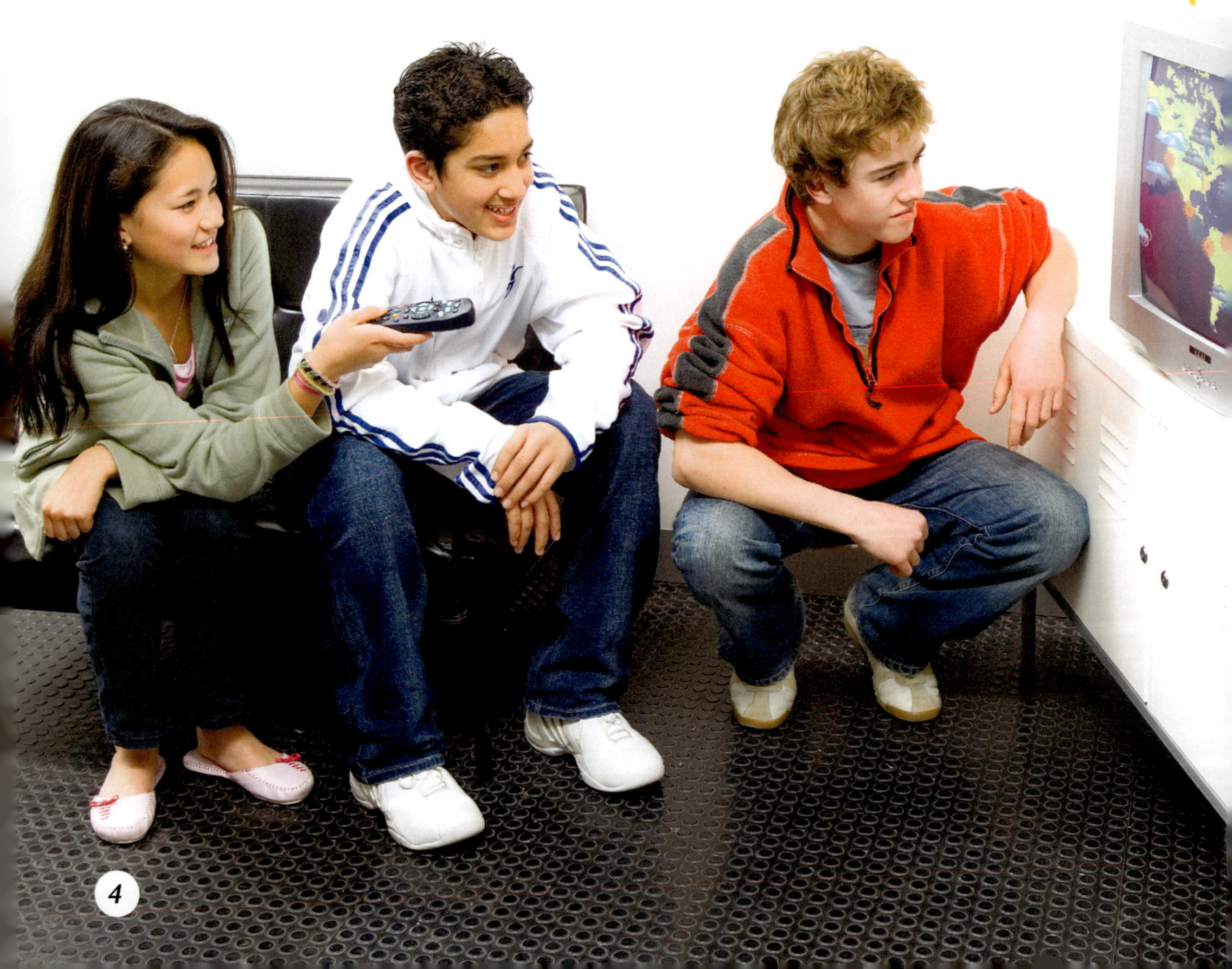

Some people go outside to see if it is hot or cold.

Anders Celsius

Temperature is measured on a scale.

There are two scales:
Celsius and **Fahrenheit**.

The Celsius scale is named after a man called Celsius. He lived from 1701–1744.

Daniel Fahrenheit

The Fahrenheit scale is named after a man called Fahrenheit. He lived from 1686–1736.

Some countries use the Celsius scale to measure temperature. Some countries use the Fahrenheit scale to measure temperature.

Chapter 2

MEASURING TEMPERATURE

This is a **thermometer**.

A thermometer measures the temperature.

Running Words 104

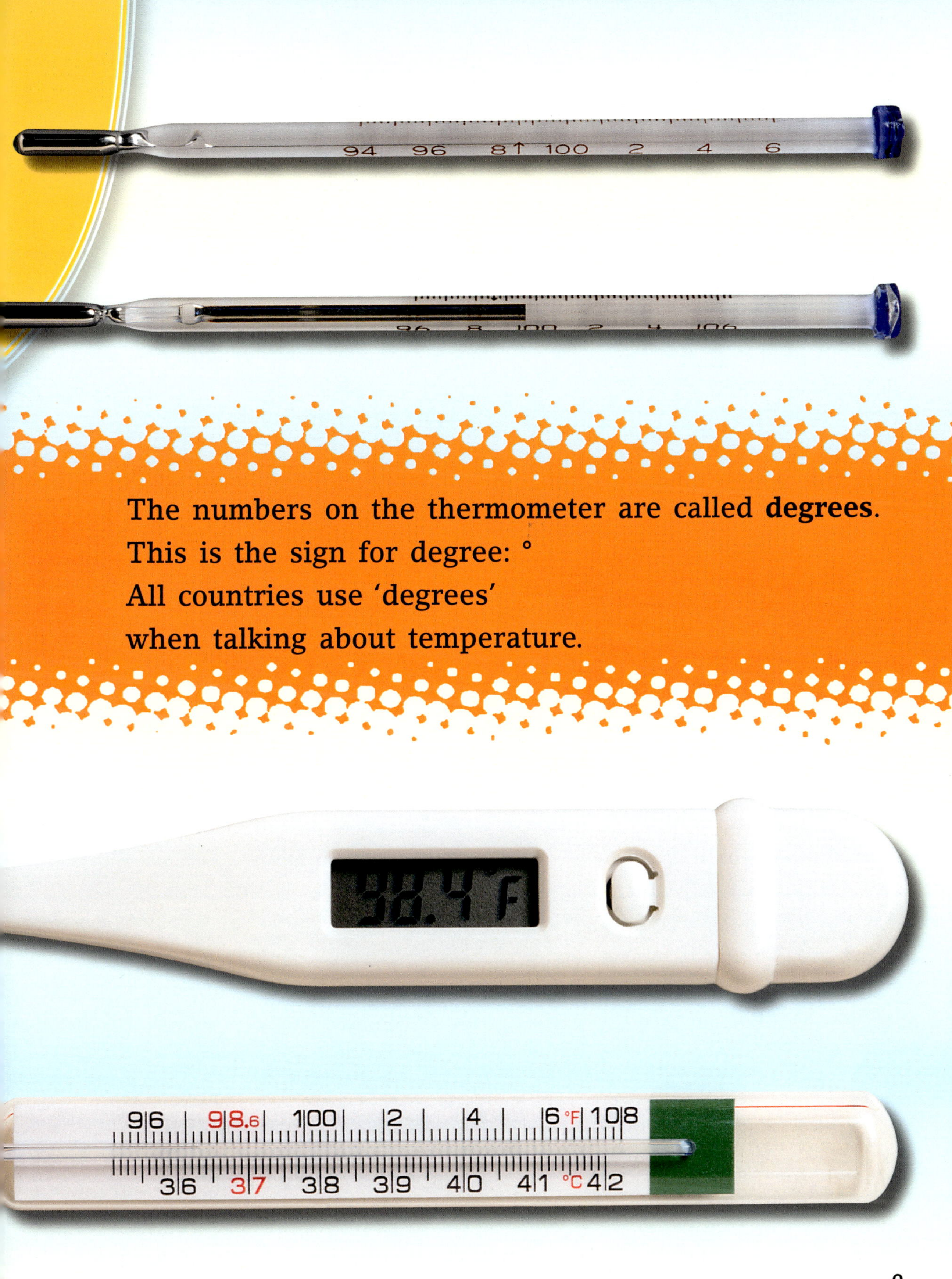

The numbers on the thermometer are called **degrees**.
This is the sign for degree: °
All countries use 'degrees'
when talking about temperature.

On the Celsius scale, water freezes at 0°.
On the Fahrenheit scale, water freezes at 32°.

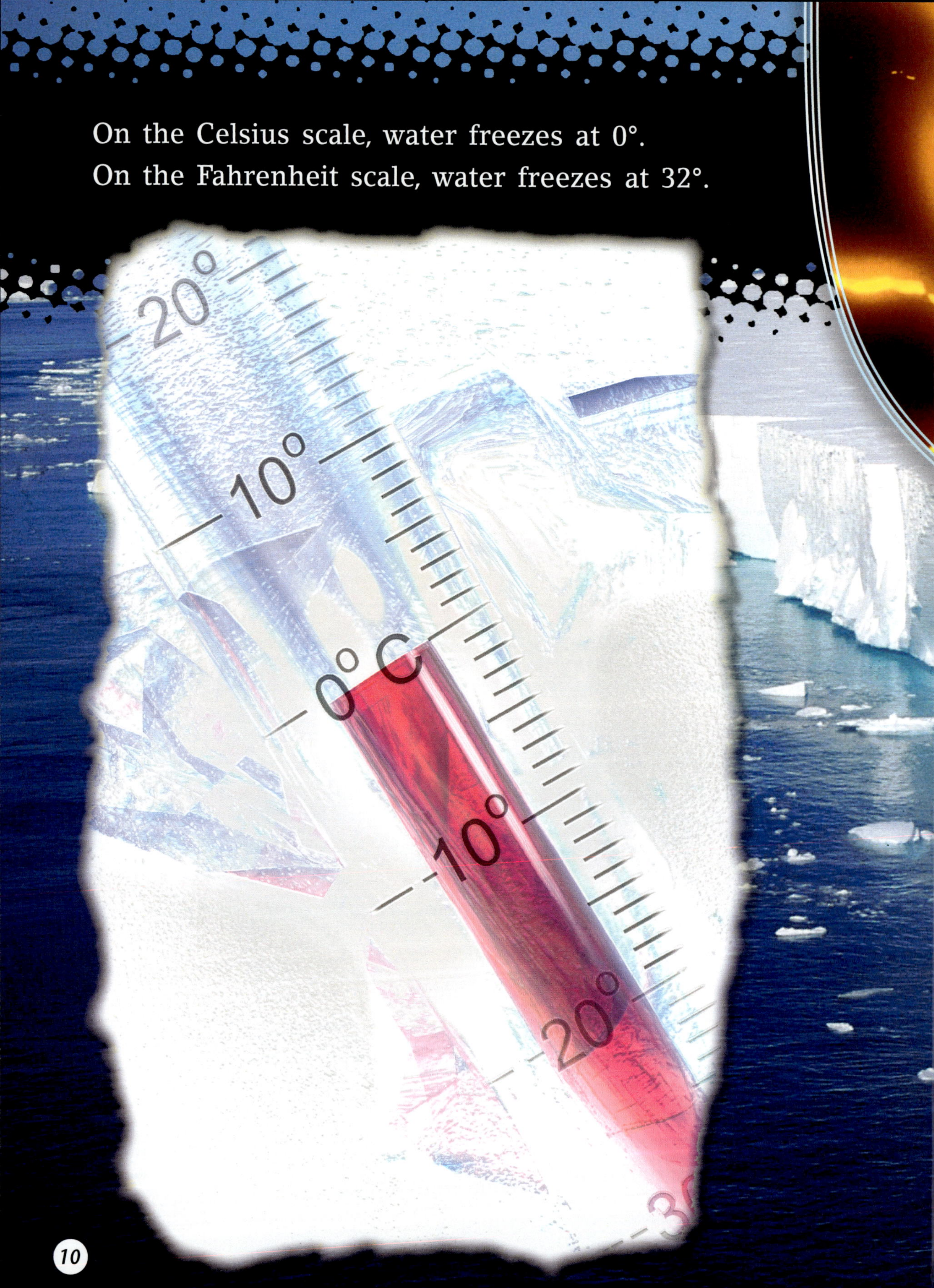

On the Celsius scale, water boils at 100°.
On the Fahrenheit scale, water boils at 212°.

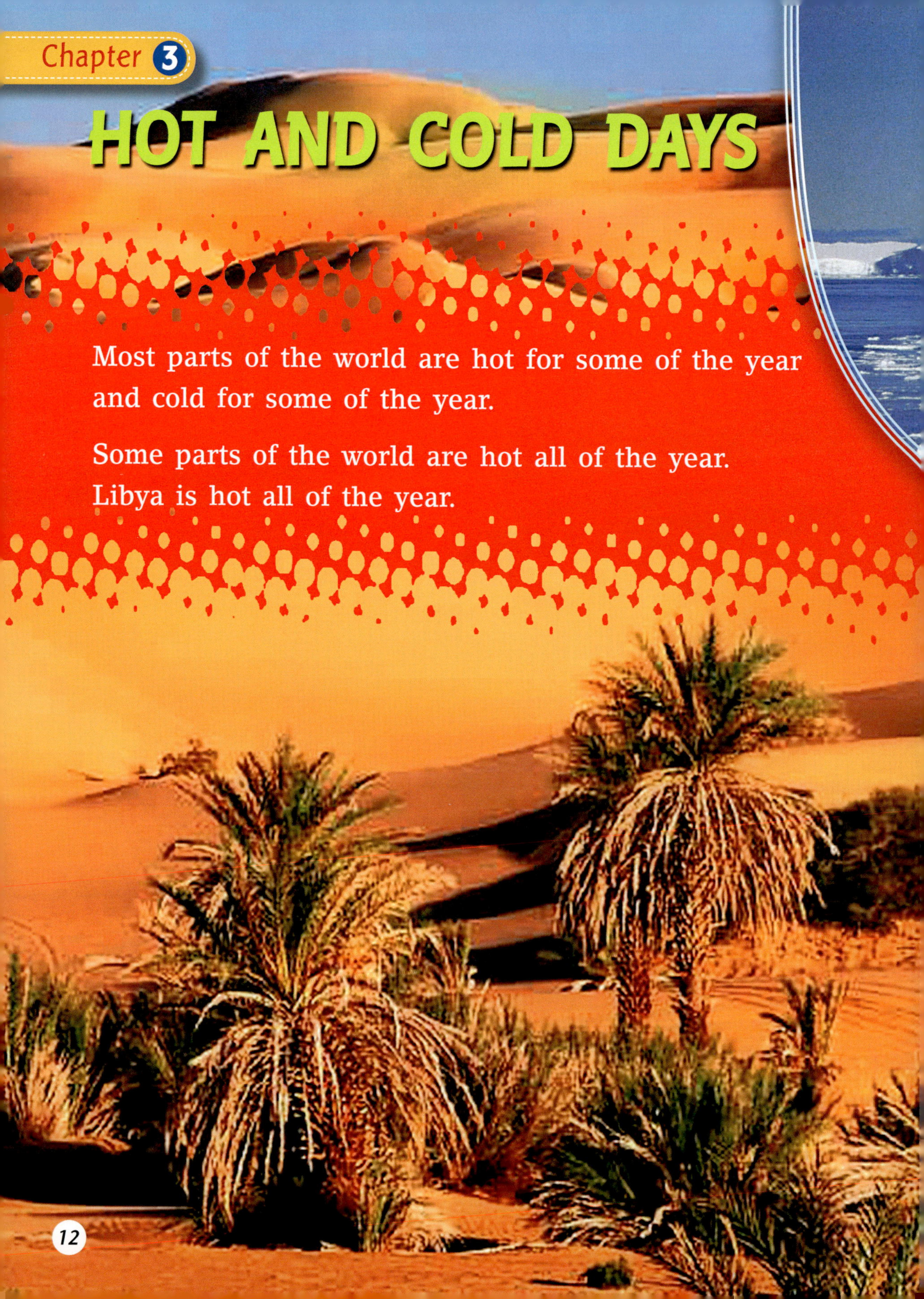

Chapter 3

HOT AND COLD DAYS

Most parts of the world are hot for some of the year and cold for some of the year.

Some parts of the world are hot all of the year. Libya is hot all of the year.

Some parts of the world are cold all of the year.
Antarctica is cold all of the year.

On 13 September 1922, a temperature of 57.3°C (136°F) was measured in Libya.
This is the hottest temperature measured in a country.

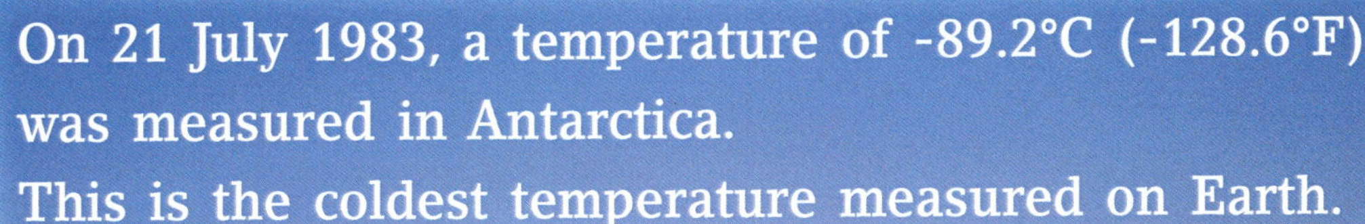

On 21 July 1983, a temperature of -89.2°C (-128.6°F) was measured in Antarctica.
This is the coldest temperature measured on Earth.

Vostock station in Antarctica

Temperature Facts

The hottest temperature measured in Australia is 50.0°C (122°F).

The coldest temperature measured in Australia is -23.0°C (-9.4°F).

The hottest temperature measured in the USA is 56.7°C (134°F).

The coldest temperature measured in the USA is -62.1°C (-79.8°F).

Glossary

Celsius	a scale to measure temperature. Water freezes at 0° Celsius.
degrees	units of measurement on a thermometer
Fahrenheit	a scale to measure temperature. Water freezes at 32° Fahrenheit.
temperature	how hot or cold something is
thermometer	an instrument that measures temperature

Index